LIFE ON THE
FRONT LINES

THE GULF WAR
ON THE FRONT LINES

by Tim Cooke

CAPSTONE PRESS
a capstone imprint

Edge Books are published by Capstone Press,
1710 Roe Crest Drive, North Mankato, Minnesota 56003
www.capstonepub.com

Published in 2014 by Capstone Publishers, Ltd.

Library of Congress Cataloging-in-Publication Data

Cooke, Tim, 1961-
The Gulf War on the front lines / by Tim Cooke.
    pages cm. -- (Edge books. Life on the front lines.)
Includes bibliographical references and index.
Summary: "Approaches the topic of the Gulf War from the perspective of
U.S. and coalition forces fighting in it"-- Provided by publisher.
Audience: Grades 4-6.
ISBN 978-1-4914-0847-6 (library binding) -- ISBN 978-1-4914-0852-0
(pbk.)
1. Persian Gulf War, 1991--Juvenile literature. I. Title.
DS79.72.C665 2015
956.7044'2--dc23

2013048931

For Brown Bear Books Ltd:
Editorial Director: Lindsey Lowe
Text: Tim Cooke
Children's Publisher: Anne O'Daly
Design Manager: Keith Davis
Designer: Lynne Lennon
Picture Manager: Sophie Mortimer
Production Director: Alastair Gourlay

Source Notes
p.9 Steven Dutch, from *Gulf War Diary*; January 7–14, 1991, "Settling Into Fort Bragg" on www.uwgb.edu/dutchs/gulfwar;
p.11 John Grifka, quoted in *The Persian Gulf War: Life of an American Soldier* by Geoffrey A. Campbell, Lucent Books, 2001,
p.14; **p.12** Norman Schwarzkopf, quoted in "War in the Gulf," *The New York Times*, 02/28/1991; **p.13** Walter S. Pullar,
quoted in the *Washington Post*, "Foreign Service" by Peter Barker, February 21, 2003, p.A19; **p.17** Clay Anderson, quoted on
Veterans History Project, interview with Clay Anderson, http://lcweb2.loc.gov/diglib/vhp/story/loc.natlib.afc2001001.00312/
transcript?ID=sr0001; **p.19** Carla Barbour-Clark, quoted in "Women Soldiers Close to Combat," *Chicago Tribune News*, January
25, 1991, www.articles.chicagotribune.com; **p.21** Roy Butler, quoted in "Gulf War Veterans in Navy Unit Tell of an Iraqi
Chemical Attack," *The New York Times* September 20, 1996; **p.23** Deborah Sheehan, quoted in *The Brave Women of the Gulf Wars:
Operation Desert Storm and Operation Iraqi Freedom* by Karen Zeinert and Mary Miller, Twenty-First Century Books, 2006, p.34;
p.27 Keith Rosenkranz, from *Vipers in the Storm* by Keith Rosenkranz, McGraw-Hill, 2002, p.105; **p.29** Corporal Saki, from
February 24, 2005, www.saki.iwarp.com.

Photo Credits
Front Cover: U.S. Department of Defense
All interior images: U.S. Department of Defense
Artistic effects: Shutterstock

Printed in China

TABLE OF CONTENTS

THE GULF WAR

In August 1990 Iraqi dictator Saddam Hussein ordered his troops to invade Iraq's tiny neighbor on the Persian Gulf, Kuwait. With authority from the United Nations, the United States organized an international **coalition** to try to force the Iraqis out of Kuwait.

U.S. troops and their allies from around the world set up a base in Saudi Arabia, a huge and wealthy oil-producing country next to Kuwait. This build-up to the war was called Operation Desert Shield.

U.S. soldiers slept in tents that each held 10 or 12 people. More than 500,000 U.S. troops took part in Operation Desert Shield.

A soldier eats in a temporary mess hall during Desert Storm. Most food was MREs, or Meals-Ready-to-Eat. The food was already prepared and just had to be heated.

The troops in Saudi Arabia were under constant threat from Iraqi missiles. It was feared that the Iraqis might use chemical weapons or poison gas. Troops in Saudi Arabia also had to put up with the desert conditions. They had to become used to living according to the traditions of an **Islamic** country.

In January 1991 coalition troops attacked the Iraqis in Kuwait. This part of the war was called Operation Desert Storm, also known as the Gulf War. The Iraqis retreated. The coalition was victorious in only two weeks.

- **coalition:** a temporary alliance of different countries formed for a specific purpose

- **Islamic:** associated with Muslim religious belief or culture

CHAPTER 1

THE MAKING OF A SOLDIER

By January 1991, 540,000 U.S. troops were stationed in the Persian Gulf. Most had never been in combat before. Troop numbers had been cut in the 1980s. The U.S. government estimated that the Iraqi Army might be as large as 1 million men, so it needed to raise troops very quickly. It called up reserve soldiers. These were civilians who had signed up to serve in a crisis.

U.S. infantrymen on a training exercise in Saudi Arabia during Operation Desert Shield, November 1990.

Infantry recruits from 1st Battalion drill with M-16A2 rifles fitted with bayonets.

Many of the reserve soldiers had special skills, such as engineering or transportation. Most did not expect to fight in a war.

In previous wars, few women had served in the U.S. armed forces. In the Gulf War around 7 percent of U.S. soldiers were women.

RECRUITMENT AND TRAINING

Expecting to be largely outnumbered by Iraqi soldiers, the U.S. Army needed to prepare large numbers of troops quickly. The first U.S. division to arrive in the Gulf was the 82nd Airborne. The division was specially trained to **deploy** at a moment's notice.

Other soldiers were quickly trained in desert survival techniques. This included how to deal with the extreme heat and the fine sand that got into everything. They learned to check for scorpions, spiders, and centipedes in their clothes. They were also taught to wear protection to shield their eyes from the sun's intense glare.

U.S. Marines hold up rifles in physical training in San Diego. Being fit helped soldiers' bodies cope with the demanding desert conditions.

Navy SEALs on a warship sailing to the Gulf fire at targets.

A drill instructor shows a recruit how to use the sight of a grenade launcher attached to his M-16 rifle.

● **deploy:** to move forces into position ready for an armed conflict

TRANSPORTATION

Kuwait is 6,500 miles (10,460 km) from Washington, D.C. All U.S. troops and equipment had to be transported to Kuwait from the United States. The hardware included 2,000 tanks, 2,200 armored personnel carriers, and 1,700 helicopters. Much of it was flown to the Gulf by plane, but some of the heaviest equipment had to be sent by ship. Supplies had to include all spare parts, fuel, and oil. Soldiers on the cargo airplanes had to fit in wherever they could around the equipment.

Soldiers from the 24th Infantry Division board a passenger plane hired by the Army. The plane was more comfortable than a transport airplane.

Troops try to rest on a crowded C-130 Hercules transport plane flying to the Gulf.

A company from 101st Airborne prepares to board a plane for the Gulf.

SPECIAL FORCES

The Gulf War saw the involvement of almost 10,000 **special forces**, the largest deployment in U.S. history. Special forces were some of the first troops in the Gulf. They carried out **reconnaissance** missions. Army Rangers helped find the way through minefields. The U.S. Air Force's First Special Operations Wing bombed Iraqi control centers. Navy SEALs seized off-coast oil installations to prevent the Iraqis from blowing them up. They also boarded suspected enemy vessels in the Persian Gulf.

An Army Ranger uses a laser projector to help U.S. bombers find their targets. The laser guided a missile to its target.

EYEWITNESS

NAME: Norman Schwarzkopf
RANK: Commander, U.S. Forces
PLACE: Kuwait

" It was a classic, absolutely classic, military breaching of a very, very tough minefield, barbed wire, fire trench-type barrier. They went through the first barrier like it was water. Then they brought both divisions steaming through that breach. Absolutely superb operation—textbook. "

Navy SEALs get training on how to board enemy vessels. One of their tasks was to enforce an **embargo** on trade with Iraq by stopping ships.

Navy SEALs and French commandos hang from a helicopter during a joint training mission.

- **special forces:** soldiers who are trained to fight in a nonconventional way, such as by ambush or other small operations

- **reconnaissance:** the military observation of an area to find out information about the enemy

- **embargo:** an international ban on all trade with a particular country

CHAPTER 2

AT THE FRONT

During Operation Desert Shield, U.S. troops were based in Saudi Arabia as they waited for the fighting to begin. Saudi Arabia lies to the south of both Kuwait and Iraq. U.S. soldiers there knew they could be attacked at any time. Iraq possessed long-range **Scud missiles**. Scuds could travel up to 180 miles (290 km) from inside Iraq to strike targets inside Saudi Arabia.

An M1A1 tank lays a smokescreen. The desert was ideal for tanks, but it was tough to keep their engines free of sand.

Most of Saudi Arabia is made up of a huge, windy sand desert. The desert was extremely hot in the day but when it got dark the temperature fell. The nights were freezing cold.

U.S. troops with a squad automatic weapon (SAW) man a **foxhole** during Desert Storm. Such a position would give cover from any Iraqi infantry attack on U.S. positions.

While in Saudi Arabia, U.S. soldiers took care not to offend their hosts. Female soldiers had to be careful to obey Islamic rules about keeping their skin and hair covered at all times. Men had to avoid innocent mistakes, such as asking Saudi men questions about their families. Such personal conversations were seen as inappropriate.

- **Scud missile:** a long-range missile used by the Iraqis; Scuds were not very accurate, and coalition forces shot down many of them

- **foxhole:** a hole in the ground that soldiers use as a firing position or for protection from enemy fire

LIVING CONDITIONS

As they waited for the fighting to begin, coalition forces turned parts of Saudi Arabia into huge military bases. The troops lived in "tent cities." Each tent had 10 or more camp beds for soldiers, who kept their belongings in small lockers. The tents got very hot during the day. Keeping clean was important to prevent disease, so soldiers put up showers. All water had to be brought in by tankers. Toilets were just seats over an open pit. The pit's contents were regularly burned to prevent the spread of disease.

This tent city was in Saudi Arabia. **Camouflage** made the tents less noticeable from the air.

- **camouflage:** colors or patterns that make objects look like their surroundings

Mess specialists serve a meal during Operation Desert Storm. Regular hot meals were a good way to keep up **morale** among the soldiers.

Sandstorms in the desert covered everything that was not protected in sand dust.

● **morale:** the fighting spirit of a person or group, and how confident he or they feel of winning a victory

UNIFORMS AND EQUIPMENT

Uniforms and weapons were suited to the conditions of the desert. Desert camouflage was tan, brown, and black. Soldiers called the colors of their uniforms "chocolate chip." Tanks and transportation vehicles were painted in similar colors. Soldiers had gas-proof suits in case of a chemical attack. Most soldiers carried an M-16A2 rifle. They also carried **Global Positioning System** (GPS) devices to tell them precisely where they were.

A soldier hangs laundry to dry above a gas stove. Tent cities had large laundry tents, but many soldiers also did their laundry by hand.

Marines strip down their guns to clean them. Weapons had to be cleaned almost daily to keep them free of sand in order to make sure they did not jam.

EYEWITNESS

NAME: Carla Barbour-Clark
RANK: Sergeant, 438th Aerial Port Squadron
PLACE: Saudi Arabia

❝ That rush of adrenaline comes and there's a moment of panic. Then I don my chem gear and help anyone who's having trouble. ❞

One way soldiers tried to get used to the heat was by moving around camp wearing their gas-proof suits and gas masks.

● **Global Positioning System:** a device that uses satellite signals to find a precise location on Earth

19

MEDICINE AND HEALTH

U.S. commanders feared many troops would be killed or wounded. The Army sent 23,000 medical personnel to the Gulf. The biggest fear was a chemical attack. All soldiers were vaccinated against deadly sarin gas. In the Gulf, they were issued protective clothing and gas masks. Further health hazards included inhaling smoke from burning oil wells. After the war, many soldiers reported symptoms such as chronic tiredness and stomach problems. This became known as Gulf War Syndrome.

U.S. Army nurses evacuate an injured Iraqi soldier by helicopter.

EYEWITNESS
NAME: Roy Butler
RANK: Petty Officer, 24th Naval Mobile Construction Battalion
PLACE: Saudi Arabia

" I put my gas mask on right away, but by the time I got to the bunker, my hands and face were burning, and I couldn't breathe. "

The crew chief of a Blackhawk helicopter from the 45th Medical Company stows a folded-up stretcher with other gear.

A combat medical team moves a soldier from a Blackhawk during training in the desert.

21

TASKS AND DUTIES

Supplies had to be unloaded, hardware had to be maintained, and soldiers had to be ready to face any threat. Many soldiers had specific jobs, such as medics or mechanics. Some were cooks in mobile canteen trucks who served hamburgers and fries. All soldiers had daily training exercises. They did fitness drills for hours, often wearing gas-proof suits and carrying packs. Motorized patrols went out into the desert to check for enemy activity. They also prepared the way for a U.S. advance into Kuwait.

A member of a Naval Construction Battalion watches the desert for signs of enemy movement.

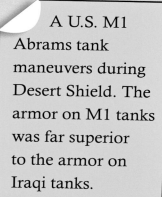

A U.S. M1 Abrams tank maneuvers during Desert Shield. The armor on M1 tanks was far superior to the armor on Iraqi tanks.

A patrol prepares to set off in Humvees. The multi-purpose vehicles were mounted with machine guns.

CHAPTER 3

SPIRIT AND MORALE

Boredom was a big problem during Desert Shield. Carrying out everyday activities, such as doing laundry, helped keep up spirits. Getting mail from home was also a huge morale booster. Thousands of people at home joined a campaign to write letters addressed to "Any American Soldier." It was reassuring for the soldiers to know that people at home supported the troops' efforts. Many people also sent the soldiers small items, such as gum or batteries.

A pastor leads a prayer service in the desert. Many soldiers in the war drew strength from their religious beliefs.

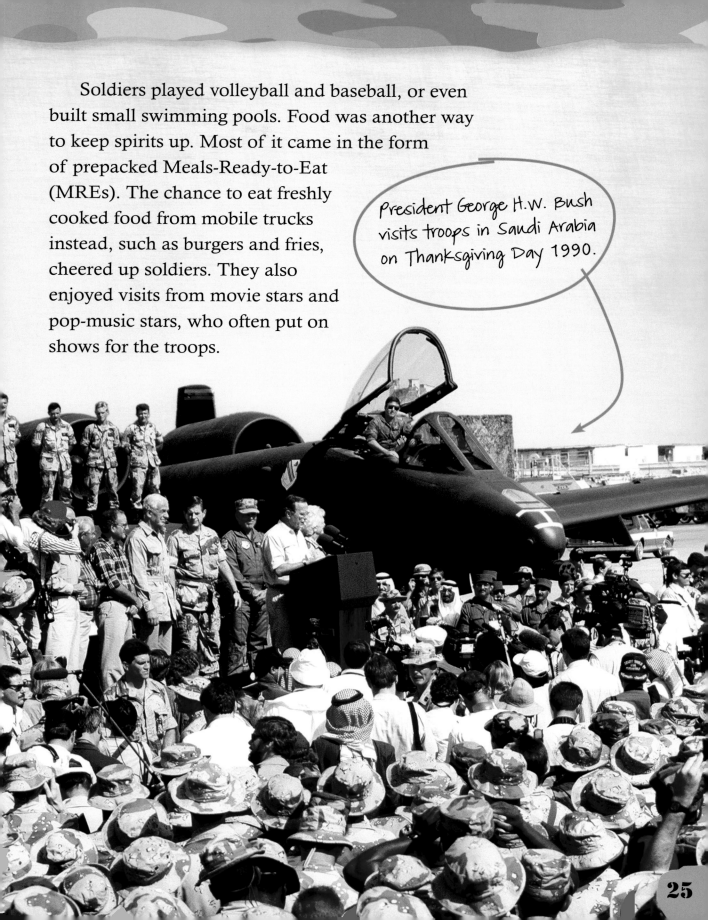

Soldiers played volleyball and baseball, or even built small swimming pools. Food was another way to keep spirits up. Most of it came in the form of prepacked Meals-Ready-to-Eat (MREs). The chance to eat freshly cooked food from mobile trucks instead, such as burgers and fries, cheered up soldiers. They also enjoyed visits from movie stars and pop-music stars, who often put on shows for the troops.

President George H.W. Bush visits troops in Saudi Arabia on Thanksgiving Day 1990.

RECREATION AND ENTERTAINMENT

Even after the soldiers had completed all their tasks, they still had a lot of time to fill by relaxing. Soldiers wrote letters and read mail or watched TV and movies. Some soldiers rigged up sophisticated entertainment centers in their tents, which were run by gas-powered generators. There were also recreation tents, which usually had pool and table-tennis tables. The soldiers also enjoyed playing ball games outdoors.

A Marine writes a letter. Staying in touch with loved ones was a priority for many soldiers living in an unfamiliar environment.

The recreation tents had table tennis, table football, and a range of arcade games.

EYEWITNESS

NAME: Capt Keith Rosenkranz
RANK: SF-16 Fighter Pilot
PLACE: KAl Minhab Airbase, Saudi Arabia

" I was touched that a group of kids who didn't know me would take the time to write... I sat in the club and read each of the letters... After finishing the last letter, I decided to write a personal note to every child. "

Celebrities such as comedian Steve Martin (left) visited troops and put on shows. Such visits had been useful in keeping up morale in previous wars.

HOMECOMING

U.S. soldiers received a heroes' welcome when they returned home after Operation Desert Storm. After the Vietnam War (1959–1975), many U.S. veterans felt unappreciated when they got home. People were determined that would not happen again after the Gulf War.

Thousands of veterans marched in New York City in what was called the "Mother of All Parades." As the troops marched along Broadway, ticker tape rained down. The joyful scene was repeated across the country as some 220 communities welcomed servicemen and servicewomen back home.

A boy holds up a newspaper during the Gulf War parade through New York City.

An Army private marches in the ticker-tape parade that welcomed veterans to New York City.

All over the country, like here on a control tower at an air wing base, signs welcomed the veterans home.

29

GLOSSARY

camouflage (KA-muh-flahzh)— colors or patterns that make objects look like their surroundings

coalition (koh-ah-LISH-un)—a temporary alliance of different countries formed for a specific purpose

deploy (dee-PLOY)—to move forces into position ready for an armed conflict

embargo (em-BAR-goh)—a ban on all trade with a particular country

foxhole (FOX-hole)—a hole in the ground that soldiers use as a firing position or for protection from enemy fire

Global Positioning System— (GLOH-buhl puh-ZI-shuh-ning SISS-tuhm): a device that uses satellite signals to find a precise location on Earth

Islamic (is-LAH-mik)—associated with Muslim religious belief or culture

maneuver (muh-NOO-ver)—a large-scale practice exercise that involves a series of coordinated moves by military forces

morale (muh-RAL)—the fighting spirit of a person or group, and how confident he or they feel of winning a victory

patrol (puh-TROHL)—a group of soldiers who keep watch over an area by traveling around it

reconnaissance (ree-KAH-nuh-suhnss)—the military observation of an area to find out information about the enemy

Scud missile (SKUD MISS-uhl)—a long-range missile used by the Iraqis; scuds were not very accurate, and coalition forces shot down many of them

special forces (spesh-UL FOR-sess)—soldiers who are trained to fight in a nonconventional way, such as by ambush or other small operations

United Nations (YOO-nite-uhd NAY-shuns)—an international organization that tries to resolve international disputes peacefully

READ MORE

Bingham, Jane. *The Gulf Wars with Iraq*. Living Through. Chicago, Ill.: Heinemann Library, 2012.

Gitlin, Martin. *Operation Desert Storm*. Essential Events. Edina, Minn.: Abdo Publishing Company, 2009.

Gregory, Josh. *The Persian Gulf War*. Cornerstones of Freedom. New York: Children's Press, 2012.

Perritano, John. *Desert Storm*. America at War. New York: Franklin Watts, 2010.

Samuels, Charlie. *Machines and Weaponry of the Gulf War*. Machines that Won the War. New York: Gareth Stevens Publishing, 2013.

INTERNET SITES

FactHound offers a safe, fun way to find Internet sites related to this book. All of the sites on FactHound have been researched by our staff.

Here's all you do:

Visit *www.facthound.com*

Type in this code: 9781491408476

 Check out projects, games and lots more at
www.capstonekids.com

INDEX